FOOTBALL'S SUPER BOWL

PERCY LEED

LERNER PUBLICATIONS ◆ MINNEAPOLIS

Lerner Publications Company
An imprint of Lerner Publishing Group, Inc.
241 First Avenue North
Minneapolis, MN 55401 USA

For reading levels and more information, look up this title at www.lernerbooks.com.

Main body text set in Mikado.
Typeface provided by HVD Fonts.

Library of Congress Cataloging-in-Publication Data

Names: Leed, Percy, 1968- author.
Title: Football's Super Bowl / Percy Leed.
Description: Minneapolis : Lerner Publications, [2025] | Series: Lerner sports rookie. Championship games | Includes bibliographical references and index. | Audience: Ages 5–8 years | Audience: Grades K–1 | Summary: "Every year, millions of fans tune in to watch the Super Bowl. From its greatest moments to its star players, young readers will enjoy learning more about football's biggest game"— Provided by publisher.
Identifiers: LCCN 2024008830 (print) | LCCN 2024008831 (ebook) | ISBN 9798765648032 (lib. bdg.) | ISBN 9798765661505 (pbk.) | ISBN 9798765653876 (epub)
Subjects: LCSH: Super Bowl—History—Juvenile literature.
Classification: LCC GV956.2.S8 L45 2025 (print) | LCC GV956.2.S8 (ebook) | DDC 796.332/648—dc23/eng/20240401

LC record available at https://lccn.loc.gov/2024008830
LC ebook record available at https://lccn.loc.gov/2024008831

Manufactured in the United States of America
1-1010912-53364-4/24/2024

TABLE OF CONTENTS

CHAPTER 1
THE BIG GAME

The Kansas City Chiefs played the San Francisco 49ers in the 2024 Super Bowl. The score was 19–19. The Chiefs won with a touchdown!

The American Football League joined the NFL in 1966. Each league's winner played in a final game. The team that won became the NFL champion.

CHAPTER 2
GREATEST MOMENTS

The 1995 Super Bowl was the highest-scoring Super Bowl of all time. The San Francisco 49ers beat the San Diego Chargers 49–26. That was a total of 75 points!

In 2015, the Seattle Seahawks had 20 seconds left in the game. They were one yard away from scoring a winning touchdown.

But the New England Patriots stopped them.

The Patriots won 28–24.

The Atlanta Falcons were ahead 28–3 against the New England Patriots in 2017. No one expected the Patriots to catch up. But they won 34–28.

CHAPTER 3
BEST PLAYERS

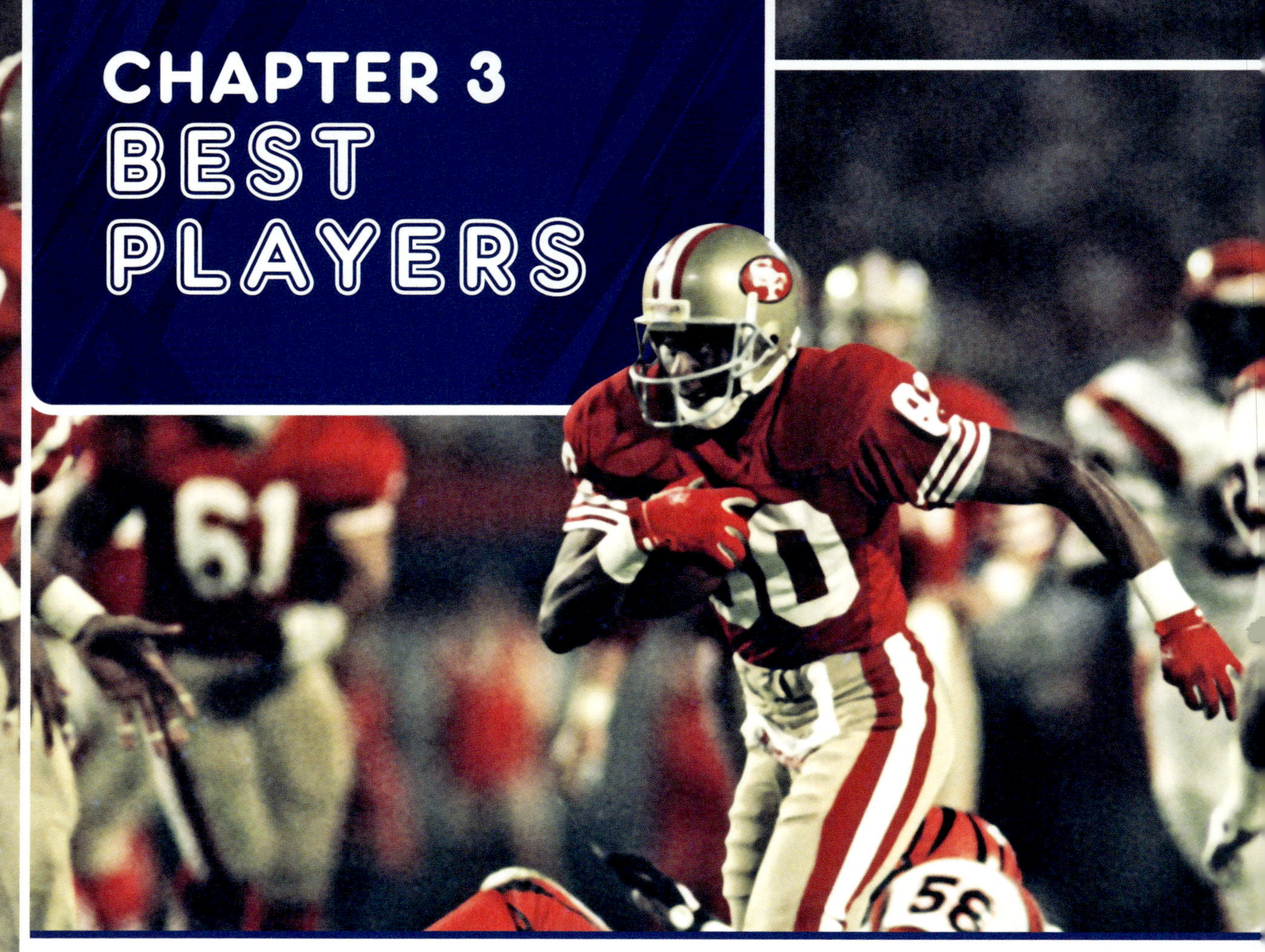

Jerry Rice is one of the best wide receivers in NFL history. In 1989, he broke the record for most receiving yards in a Super Bowl game.

Running back Terrell Davis had both speed and power. He received the Most Valuable Player award in 1998.

Quarterback Patrick Mahomes led the Kansas City Chiefs to four Super Bowls. He won three of them.

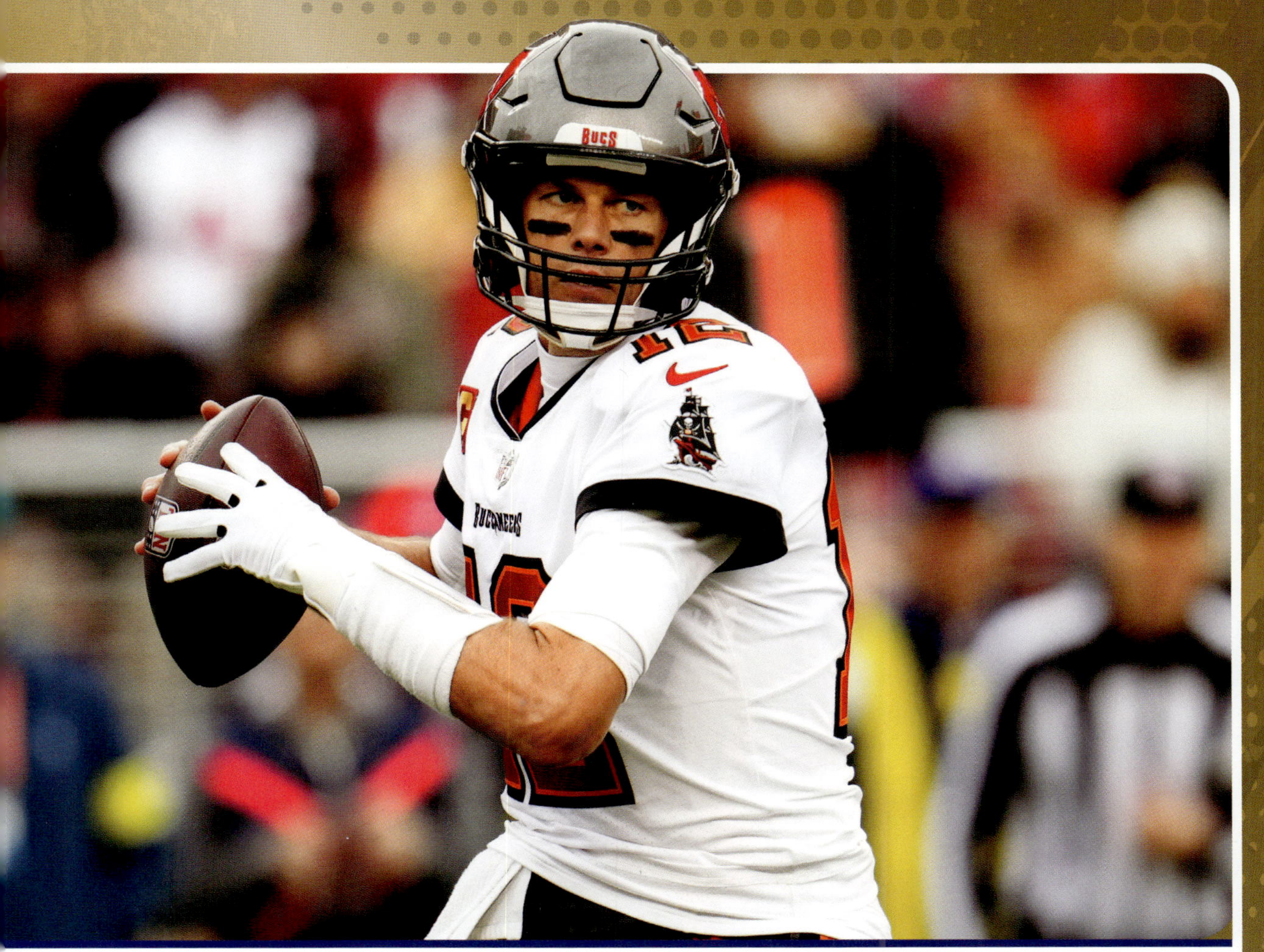

No player has won more Super Bowls than Tom Brady. He went to 10 Super Bowls and won seven of them.

CHAPTER 4
GAME DAY

Thousands of fans fill the stadium for the Super Bowl. Bands play songs and people cheer.

Top singers such as Rihanna perform at halftime.

People can watch the game from home with friends and family. No matter who wins, the Super Bowl is fun and exciting!

CHAMPIONS
NFL
15
NKH

SUPER BOWL CHAMPS

Here are recent Super Bowl winners!

2024 Kansas City Chiefs

2023 Kansas City Chiefs

2022 Los Angeles Rams

2021 Tampa Bay Buccaneers

2020 Kansas City Chiefs

2019 New England Patriots

2018 Philadelphia Eagles

2017 New England Patriots

2016 Denver Broncos

2015 New England Patriots

FUN FACTS

The 2024 Super Bowl is the most watched Super Bowl of all time with 123 million viewers.

The New England Patriots and Pittsburgh Steelers have both won six Super Bowls.

In 2024, the price of an average Super Bowl ticket was more than $8,600.

GLOSSARY

field goal: a score of three points made by kicking the ball over the crossbar

NFL: short for National Football League

receiving yard: a yard gained by a player after catching a pass

Super Bowl: the NFL's championship game

LEARN MORE

Goodman, Michael E. *Kansas City Chiefs*. Mankato, MN: Creative Education, 2023.

Hansen, Grace. *Tom Brady: NFL Great and Super Bowl MVP.* Minneapolis: Abdo Kids, 2022.

Leed, Percy. *Football: A First Look*. Minneapolis: Lerner Publications, 2021.

INDEX

PHOTO ACKNOWLEDGMENTS

Image credits: Ezra Shaw/Getty Images, pp. 4–5; Walter Iooss Jr./Getty Images, p. 7; Joseph Patronite/Getty Images, pp. 8–9; Tom Hauck/Getty Images, p. 10; Focus On Sport/Getty Images, pp. 11–12, 19; Rick Stewart/Stringer/Getty Images, pp. 14–15; Vincent Laforet/Getty Images, p. 15; David Eulitt/Stringer/Getty Images, p. 16; Cooper Neill/Getty Images, p. 17; Erick W. Rasco/Getty Images, pp. 18–19; Perry Knotts/Getty Images, p. 21.
Design element: Winner Creative/Shutterstock. Cover: AP Photo/Doug Benc.